SUBSTANCE ABUSE RECOVERY ACTIVITIES FOR FAMILIES

Healing Beyond Addiction: Practical Steps for Families on the Road to Recovery, Effective Tools, Building Stronger Bonds and Strategies

George Leo

DEDICATION

To families going through the challenges of substance abuse, this book is dedicated to your strength, resilience, and love. May it serve as a source of hope, understanding, and healing as you rebuild together.

ACKNOWLEDGMENTS

I deeply thank my family for their unwavering encouragement and patience throughout this process. To the experts and professionals who generously shared their insights, your guidance was invaluable. To my readers, your trust fuels this effort. This book exists because of the support, love, and belief of those around me.

TABLE OF CONTENTS

INTRODUCTION

Substance abuse doesn't just affect the individual; it disrupts entire families, leaving a trail of confusion, pain, and broken trust. The struggle of watching a loved one battle addiction can feel isolating, and the damage it causes often goes unnoticed, hidden behind the façade of normalcy. However, healing is possible—not just for the person struggling with addiction, but for the family as a whole. **Substance Abuse Recovery Activities for Families** offers practical solutions for families facing this challenging reality. It highlights the importance of open communication, setting healthy boundaries, and finding support to rebuild trust and understanding. This book provides actionable steps, resources, and strategies to empower families to take charge of their healing, bringing strength and unity where there was once despair. It's a guide to help families turn their pain into progress, creating a path to a healthier, more connected future.

PART 1: UNDERSTANDING SUBSTANCE ABUSE AND ITS IMPACT

CHAPTER 1

WHAT IS SUBSTANCE ABUSE?

Substance abuse refers to the harmful or hazardous use of psychoactive substances, including alcohol and drugs, to the point where it interferes with a person's life. It is a condition marked by an individual's dependence on substances, where the need to use them often overrides personal, professional, and social responsibilities. Substance abuse is not limited to illegal drugs; it also includes prescription medication misuse, alcohol, and other legal substances that are abused.

At the core of substance abuse is addiction, which is the physical and psychological compulsion to keep using a substance, despite negative consequences. Addiction is not a sign of weakness; it is a complex disease that affects both the brain and behavior. In fact, addiction changes the brain's chemistry, affecting areas responsible for judgment, decision-making, memory, and the ability to experience pleasure. This makes overcoming addiction extremely difficult for the person involved, but with support and proper treatment, recovery is possible.

Defining Substance Abuse and Addiction

Substance abuse and addiction often coexist, but they are distinct in their nature. Substance abuse refers to the misuse of substances, while addiction signifies a deeper level of dependency, where the person becomes physically and psychologically reliant on the substance. Both conditions are harmful, but addiction tends to be more severe and involves long-term patterns of behavior that can impact every aspect of an individual's life.

Addiction doesn't happen overnight. It often develops gradually, starting with casual or recreational use that leads to tolerance. As the body becomes used to the substance, the person needs higher doses to achieve the same effect, which increases the risk of dependence. Over time, individuals may find themselves unable to control their use, and their lives begin to revolve around obtaining and using the substance.

Common Signs of Addiction in Loved Ones

Recognizing addiction in a loved one is crucial to offering help before the situation worsens. Addiction manifests differently in each person, but there are several common signs that may indicate someone is struggling with substance abuse:

1. **Behavioral Changes**: A loved one may begin to exhibit erratic behavior, become secretive, or act in ways that are inconsistent with their usual character. They might withdraw from social activities and relationships that were once important to them.

2. **Physical Changes**: Substance abuse can lead to noticeable changes in appearance. These include weight fluctuations, bloodshot eyes, poor hygiene, and unusual body odors. Chronic use can also result in skin problems, such as sores or paleness.

3. **Financial Issues**: People with substance abuse problems often experience financial strain. They may ask for loans, sell possessions, or engage in risky behaviors to fund their addiction.

4. **Mood Swings**: Addiction often causes extreme mood swings. The individual may experience irritability, anxiety, or even depression when not using the substance. They may become defensive or angry when questioned about their behavior or habits.

5. **Neglecting Responsibilities**: A person struggling with addiction may neglect their work, school, or family responsibilities. They may show up late or miss important commitments due to their need to use substances.

6. **Physical Dependence**: A loved one may exhibit withdrawal symptoms such as shaking, sweating, or nausea when not using the substance. This physical dependence often escalates as tolerance increases, and the person may use the substance just to feel "normal" or avoid discomfort.

7. **Loss of Control**: Even if the person expresses a desire to quit, they may find it impossible to stop using the substance on their own. They may try to cut down but end up using more, revealing the depth of their dependency.

Why Addiction Affects the Entire Family

Substance abuse is a family issue, not just an individual problem. The effects of addiction extend far beyond the person using the substance. It can significantly impact family dynamics, create emotional strain, and cause long-term damage to relationships. Understanding how addiction affects the entire family can help loved ones better support the individual and begin the process of healing.

1. **Emotional Toll**: Family members often experience intense emotional stress. The person with addiction may behave unpredictably, causing anxiety, anger, and confusion. The emotional rollercoaster of hope followed by disappointment can wear down family members, leaving them feeling helpless or isolated.

2. **Financial Strain**: Addiction often leads to financial problems. Family members may find themselves covering for the addicted person's lack of responsibility, paying off debts, or financing their substance use. This can lead to resentment, frustration, and even financial ruin in some cases.

3. **Broken Trust**: Trust is often broken when addiction takes hold. The individual with the addiction may lie, hide their behaviors, or manipulate family members to cover up their actions. This can create a toxic environment where

communication breaks down, and relationships deteriorate.

4. **Impact on Children**: Children of parents with substance abuse issues often bear the brunt of the emotional and psychological consequences. These children may grow up in an unstable environment, experiencing neglect, abuse, or emotional abandonment. They may develop mental health problems, have difficulty forming healthy relationships, or even struggle with addiction themselves as they grow older.

5. **Codependency**: In many families, especially those where one member is struggling with addiction, the concept of codependency develops. This happens when family members enable the addicted person's behavior by providing financial support, covering up for them or making excuses. Codependency can prevent the individual from

seeking help and make it harder for the family to break free from the cycle of addiction.

6. **Physical and Mental Health Struggles**: Dealing with an addicted family member can lead to stress-related physical and mental health problems. Family members often suffer from anxiety, depression, insomnia, or other stress-related illnesses. The constant worry about the well-being of the person with addiction can take a significant toll on their health.

7. **Social Isolation**: The stigma of addiction can lead to social isolation. Families may distance themselves from friends and other relatives due to embarrassment or shame. This isolation can make it harder for the family to find the support they need and can leave them feeling alone in their struggles.

8. **Disruption of Family Roles**: The family dynamic is often disrupted when one member is struggling with addiction. In some cases, children may have to take on adult roles, such as caring for younger

siblings or taking over household responsibilities. In others, the addicted person may dominate the family's attention, leaving others to fend for themselves emotionally.

CHAPTER 2

THE IMPACT OF ADDICTION ON FAMILY DYNAMICS

Addiction's effect on family dynamics is profound, often reshaping relationships, shifting roles, and creating deep emotional scars. As the addictive behavior takes root in one family member, it gradually permeates the entire family system, causing dysfunction and confusion. But this doesn't have to be the end of the story. With understanding, support, and proactive solutions, families can heal and rebuild their connections. Addressing the impact of addiction on family dynamics involves tackling specific problems, such as broken communication, codependency, and the roles family members unknowingly play in sustaining or mitigating the addiction.

Solving the Problem of Broken Communication

One of the most pervasive and damaging consequences of addiction is broken communication within the family. When a family member is struggling with substance abuse, honest and open conversations become increasingly difficult. Addiction often leads to secrecy, denial, and dishonesty, creating a wall between the person with the addiction and their loved ones. This communication breakdown prevents understanding, fosters resentment, and prevents any real solutions from being put in place.

To solve this problem, the first step is acknowledging the breakdown and recognizing that communication must be restored for the family to heal. The following strategies can help:

1. **Create a Safe Space for Honest Dialogue**: Family members need to know they can express their feelings without fear of judgment, anger, or rejection. Setting aside time for honest and open discussions, where every person is allowed to speak their truth, is vital. This should be done in a calm and neutral setting, away from triggers, where the addicted person doesn't feel accused or attacked.

2. **Listen Actively and Empathetically**: Communication isn't just about speaking—it's about listening, too. Listening actively means hearing beyond the words and trying to understand the emotions and underlying fears behind what's being said. For family members of an addicted individual, this is crucial. Often, the addiction becomes an outlet for deeper, unresolved issues such as trauma, stress, or feelings of inadequacy. When family members listen with empathy, they begin to recognize that the addiction is a symptom, not the root problem.

3. **Use "I" Statements Rather Than "You" Accusations**: One of the most common causes of communication breakdown in families affected by addiction is the accusatory tone that often emerges. Statements like "You never listen" or "You always lie" can make the addicted person feel cornered and defensive. Instead, encourage family members to use "I" statements—such as "I feel hurt when you hide things from me" or "I'm scared when I don't know where you are"—to express emotions without blaming or attacking.

4. **Set Boundaries and Stay Consistent**: Communication often becomes toxic when family members are unsure of how to respond to the addicted person's behavior. Enabling, or making excuses for someone's actions, creates confusion and undermines trust. By setting clear, consistent boundaries, families can rebuild trust and establish healthier interactions. For instance, if a family

member promises to go to rehab and fails to follow through, it's important for others to express their disappointment and let the individual know the consequences of their actions.

5. **Seek Professional Help**: Addiction often requires the expertise of a therapist or counselor to help facilitate open communication. Family therapy can provide a structured environment where family members can express their feelings and work through difficult issues. Having a neutral third party can prevent the situation from escalating into arguments or emotional outbursts, making it easier to find solutions together.

How Addiction Causes Codependency and Enabling

One of the most insidious dynamics that addiction breeds within families is codependency. Codependency is a dysfunctional behavioral pattern where one person in the relationship (often a family member) sacrifices their own needs, emotions, and well-being in order to protect, rescue, or enable the person with the addiction. This dynamic is often born from a sense of love or obligation, but it ultimately makes it more difficult for the addicted person to get the help they need and perpetuates a cycle of unhealthy behavior.

Codependent behavior can take many forms, including:

1. **Making Excuses**: Codependent family members often make excuses for the addicted person's behavior, such as covering up their absence from work, lying about their whereabouts, or minimizing the consequences of their actions. By enabling the addiction, they prevent the person from facing the full reality of their behavior, which can delay the realization that they need help.

2. **Rescuing the Addicted Person**: This often involves stepping in to take care of practical

matters that the addicted person neglects. For instance, a spouse may pay the bills or handle legal problems caused by the addiction. While this may seem like helping, it actually prevents the addicted person from feeling the full weight of their actions, and may even enable them to continue using substances without facing real-world consequences.

3. **Constantly Sacrificing Own Needs:** Codependent individuals often put the needs of the addicted person ahead of their own well-being. They may neglect their own emotional needs, health, and sometimes even their safety, in order to take care of the addicted family member. This leads to burnout, resentment, and an overall sense of helplessness.

4. **Avoiding Conflict:** Many codependent family members avoid confrontation at all costs, even when it's necessary. They may avoid discussing the addiction or enabling behavior because they fear causing conflict, triggering an emotional reaction,

or pushing the person further away. This avoidance makes it impossible to address the problem in a productive way.

Breaking the Cycle of Codependency

The first step in breaking the cycle of codependency is recognizing the behavior and its impact. It's crucial for family members to understand that their desire to help the addicted person may be coming from a place of love, but it is often counterproductive. Codependency keeps the addicted person from taking responsibility for their actions and seeking real help.

Here are some steps to overcome codependency:

1. **Set Clear Boundaries**: Family members need to establish and maintain boundaries that prioritize their own health and well-being. This can include refusing to bail someone out of jail or not providing money for substances. Boundaries allow

the addicted person to experience the natural consequences of their behavior, which may encourage them to seek help.

2. **Seek Therapy**: Therapy is an important tool in addressing codependency. Individual therapy can help family members understand why they engage in codependent behaviors, while family therapy can help the entire family heal and learn healthier ways of relating to each other.

3. **Focus on Self-Care**: Family members should learn to prioritize their own needs and well-being. This might include setting aside time for personal hobbies, developing a support system of friends or other family members, or even engaging in mindfulness or stress-relief techniques.

Understanding Roles Family Members Play in Addiction

In many families, addiction results in shifting roles that affect the family unit. These roles, often subconscious, play a critical part in perpetuating or breaking the cycle of addiction. The most common roles include:

1. **The Addicted Person**: This individual is the focal point of the addiction. They may act as though the addiction is the only thing that defines them, and may try to control the family's behavior through manipulation or guilt. However, underneath the addiction, the person is often struggling with their own pain and fears.

2. **The Enabler**: As discussed, the enabler (often a spouse, parent, or sibling) tries to protect the addicted person from facing the consequences of their behavior. They might make excuses for the addicted person or take on extra responsibilities to prevent problems from arising. While their intentions may come from a place of love, enabling only sustains the addiction.

3. **The Scapegoat**: Often, another family member becomes the "scapegoat" in an attempt to deflect

attention from the addicted person. This individual may act out, rebel, or engage in self-destructive behavior as a way of coping with the chaos caused by addiction. They may feel neglected or misunderstood, and often receive the blame for problems within the family.

4. **The Hero**: The "hero" is the family member who tries to compensate for the dysfunction caused by the addiction. They may excel in school, work, or other areas of life, trying to create a perfect image of the family to the outside world. While this may appear like a strength, it is often a way to mask the pain and dysfunction at home.

5. **The Lost Child**: The lost child often retreats inwardly, avoiding conflict and seeking solace in isolation. They may withdraw from family interactions and become emotionally distant. This role may be taken on by a child or a partner who feels powerless in the face of the addiction.

6. **The Caregiver**: Sometimes, family members take on the role of the caregiver, trying to "fix" the

addicted person. This may involve providing emotional support, physical care, or even financial assistance. While the desire to care for a loved one is natural, it can enable the addiction and prevent the addicted person from taking responsibility for their own healing.

CHAPTER 3

THE SCIENCE OF ADDICTION AND RECOVERY

Understanding the science behind addiction and recovery is essential for breaking through the misconceptions that often surround the topic. For many, addiction is seen simply as a lack of willpower or moral failing. However, research has shown that addiction is a complex disease that impacts the brain, behavior, and physical health of individuals. Overcoming addiction is not merely about stopping the substance use; it is a comprehensive process that involves addressing the changes in the brain, engaging in therapy, and often utilizing medical support. Recovery is possible, but it requires a combination of knowledge, support, and a commitment to long-term change.

Solving the Misunderstandings about Addiction

Addiction has long been misunderstood, often stigmatized as a personal choice or a lack of discipline. This misunderstanding has led to ineffective responses and a lack of empathy toward those struggling with addiction. Breaking through these myths is vital to understanding that addiction is not just a series of bad decisions; it is a disease that affects both the mind and body.

Common Misconceptions about Addiction:

1. **Addiction is a Lack of Willpower**: One of the most harmful misconceptions is that addiction is simply a matter of willpower or self-control. In reality, addiction alters the brain's chemistry and functioning, making it extremely difficult for an

individual to simply stop using substances on their own. The need for substances can become overpowering, regardless of the individual's desires or intentions.

2. **Addicts Are Weak or Bad People**: Addiction is often associated with moral weakness or character flaws, but this is a harmful and inaccurate view. People who become addicted are often facing underlying issues such as trauma, mental health disorders, or chronic stress. Addiction is a coping mechanism that takes root over time, often as a way to deal with emotional pain or psychological distress.

3. **Recovery is Just About Stopping Use**: While quitting substances is a critical first step, recovery is a much broader process. It involves not just stopping the use of substances, but also addressing the mental, emotional, and behavioral aspects of addiction. Recovery is about healing the brain, rebuilding relationships, and learning healthier coping strategies.

4. **Relapse Means Failure**: Many people view relapse as a sign that recovery has failed, but this is not the case. Relapse is common in addiction recovery and can be part of the process of overcoming addiction. It does not mean that recovery is impossible; instead, it is an opportunity to learn more about what triggered the relapse and how to prevent it in the future.

Correcting These Misunderstandings:

Education is key in solving these misconceptions. By fostering understanding about the biology and psychology of addiction, we can shift the conversation toward one of support and empathy. Addiction is a medical condition that demands care and support, not criticism. Providing individuals with the tools to understand their addiction—and the science behind it—can empower them to take control of their recovery.

How Addiction Changes the Brain

Addiction fundamentally alters the brain, making it difficult for individuals to control their behavior even when they want to. This change is not just a matter of willpower, but a result of long-term substance use that rewires the brain's reward system. Understanding how addiction impacts the brain can help both those struggling with addiction and their loved ones appreciate the complexity of the condition and the challenges involved in recovery.

The Brain's Reward System:

The brain has a built-in system that rewards behaviors essential for survival—eating, social bonding, and procreation—by releasing dopamine, a neurotransmitter associated with pleasure and reward. When a person uses substances like drugs or alcohol, the brain's reward system is hijacked, and an overwhelming flood of dopamine is released. This flood of dopamine creates feelings of euphoria, and over time, the brain becomes accustomed to this heightened state of pleasure. The addicted person may continue to use substances in an attempt to recreate this experience.

Changes in Brain Structure and Function:

1. **Increased Tolerance**: As the brain adjusts to the presence of substances, it becomes less sensitive to dopamine, meaning that the individual requires more of the substance to achieve the same effect. This is why individuals who are addicted often escalate their use over time. Their brains have essentially "reprogrammed" themselves to rely on the substance for a pleasurable feeling.

2. **Compromised Decision-Making**: Chronic drug or alcohol use alters the prefrontal cortex, the part of the brain responsible for decision-making, impulse control, and judgment. This disruption makes it harder for individuals to make rational

decisions, resist cravings, or understand the negative consequences of their actions. The desire for immediate pleasure outweighs the ability to think long-term.

3. **Memory and Learning**: Addiction also affects the hippocampus, the brain region involved in memory and learning. This means that addictive behaviors become ingrained over time, and the brain starts to associate certain triggers or situations with substance use. These associations make it difficult for individuals to break free from addictive patterns, as they are constantly reminded of the substance use through cues in their environment.

4. **Physical Dependency**: Over time, the brain becomes physically dependent on the substance, leading to withdrawal symptoms when the substance is no longer present. These symptoms can range from mild (such as irritability or fatigue) to severe (such as seizures or hallucinations), depending on the substance and the extent of the

addiction. This physical dependency can make it even harder to quit, as the individual experiences both psychological cravings and physical discomfort.

The Role of Neuroplasticity in Recovery:

The brain is capable of change, even after long-term addiction. Neuroplasticity is the brain's ability to make new connections and change itself based on what it learns and experiences. Through treatment and recovery, the brain can heal, and healthier pathways can be developed. This process takes time, but with consistent effort, the brain's reward system can recalibrate, and individuals can begin to regain control over their behaviors. Recovery is about rewiring the brain's responses to triggers and reinforcing positive behaviors.

The Role of Therapy and Medical Support in Recovery

Addiction is not something that can typically be overcome alone. Recovery often requires both psychological and medical intervention. Therapy and medical support are key components in the recovery process, as they address the underlying causes of addiction, help individuals develop new coping skills, and manage withdrawal symptoms or cravings.

Psychotherapy and Behavioral Therapy:

1. **Cognitive Behavioral Therapy (CBT)**: CBT is a highly effective treatment for addiction. It helps individuals identify negative thought patterns that lead to substance use and develop healthier ways of thinking. Through CBT, individuals learn to manage triggers, avoid relapse, and develop coping strategies to deal with stress, anxiety, or depression—issues that often fuel substance use.

2. **Motivational Interviewing (MI)**: MI is a counseling approach that helps individuals explore their ambivalence about addiction and find their own reasons for recovery. It emphasizes the importance of the individual's autonomy in the recovery process and aims to strengthen their motivation to change.

3. **Family Therapy**: Addiction does not affect just the individual; it impacts the whole family. Family therapy helps loved ones understand addiction, improve communication, and develop healthier dynamics. Family involvement can strengthen support systems and provide a safe space for everyone to heal.

4. **Group Therapy**: Group therapy provides individuals with the opportunity to share experiences, learn from others, and build a sense of community. Support groups, like Narcotics Anonymous (NA) or Alcoholics Anonymous

(AA), offer a space for individuals to discuss their struggles and progress in a non-judgmental setting. The support and understanding from others in similar situations can be incredibly empowering.

Medical Support and Medication-Assisted Treatment (MAT)

1. **Detoxification:** This is usually the first step in recovery, where the body removes the harmful substance. Depending on the substance, detox can be dangerous and even life-threatening. Medical supervision is essential to ensure the process is safe, and medications may be administered to manage withdrawal symptoms.

2. **Medications for Cravings and Withdrawal**: In some cases, medications are used to help manage cravings and withdrawal symptoms. For example, methadone or buprenorphine may be used in the treatment of opioid addiction to reduce cravings and ease withdrawal. Similarly, disulfiram and acamprosate are medications used in the

treatment of alcohol addiction to discourage drinking and help individuals maintain sobriety.

3. **Long-Term Medication for Recovery**: For some individuals, long-term medication is necessary to maintain recovery. Medications like naltrexone or topiramate can help reduce cravings and prevent relapse. These medications, combined with therapy and support, can offer individuals the tools they need to sustain long-term sobriety.

Finally, addiction is a complex, multifaceted disease that changes the brain and impacts every aspect of a person's life. Overcoming addiction requires more than just willpower; it involves understanding the science behind addiction, addressing psychological and behavioral patterns, and using both therapy and medical support. The encouraging news is that recovery is achievable. With the right treatment and support, individuals can heal, regain control of their lives, and break free from the grip of addiction. Understanding the science of addiction—and the recovery process—empowers individuals and families to approach the issue with compassion, knowledge, and hope for the future.

PART 2: CREATING A SUPPORTIVE ENVIRONMENT FOR RECOVERY

CHAPTER 4

BUILDING A FOUNDATION FOR HEALING

Creating a supportive environment for recovery is essential for overcoming addiction and maintaining long-term sobriety. Recovery is more than just avoiding substances; it's about healing on an emotional, mental, and physical level. This process requires a foundation built on trust, healthy boundaries, and effective communication. For both the person in recovery and their loved ones, understanding how to navigate these critical areas can make all the difference in sustaining progress and fostering a safe, supportive space for healing.

Solving the Problem of Broken Trust

Trust is often the first casualty in the wake of addiction. Lies, broken promises, and repeated behaviors can erode trust between the addicted person and their family, friends, and colleagues. When someone in recovery is trying to rebuild their life, the challenge of re-establishing trust can seem overwhelming. However, it is not an impossible task. Rebuilding trust is a gradual process that requires consistency, transparency, and patience from all parties involved.

How Addiction Erodes Trust: Addiction often leads to dishonesty, secrecy, and unreliable behavior. Loved ones may have been lied to, manipulated, or betrayed, and these experiences can make it difficult to believe that the person in recovery can change. Trust is built on a history of consistent, positive actions, but in the context of addiction, that history has been marred by the destructive patterns of substance use. The emotional impact of this betrayal can lead to feelings of hurt, anger, and disappointment, making it difficult to offer forgiveness or support.

Steps to Rebuilding Trust:

1. **Take Responsibility and Be Honest**: The first step in rebuilding trust is for the person in recovery to take full responsibility for their actions. This means acknowledging the hurt they've caused and being transparent about their past behavior. While it may be difficult, honest communication is key to beginning the process of healing. Apologizing sincerely, without justifications or excuses, can help mend some of the emotional wounds caused by addiction.

2. **Be consistent:** Trust is restored gradually through steady and reliable actions. This means showing up when promised, being reliable, and demonstrating responsibility in everyday actions. Trust isn't

restored overnight; it's the small, consistent choices made every day that signal to loved ones that the person in recovery is serious about change.

3. **Set Realistic Expectations**: Rebuilding trust takes time, and both the person in recovery and their loved ones need to set realistic expectations. Understand that trust will not be restored instantly, and the road to recovery will have setbacks. Both sides must be patient, acknowledging that progress will be incremental and that setbacks are a natural part of the process.

4. **Open the Door to Forgiveness**: For loved ones, forgiving doesn't mean forgetting or condoning past behavior—it means releasing the hold that anger, hurt, or betrayal has on their emotional well-being. Forgiveness opens the door to healing, allowing both parties to move forward without the heavy burden of resentment. It is a process that

takes time and requires vulnerability, but it is an essential step for rebuilding relationships.

5. **Getting professional:** This can be crucial, as rebuilding trust can be tough, particularly when the hurt is deep. Family therapy or individual counseling can provide a safe space for both the person in recovery and their loved ones to process the emotional impacts of addiction. A therapist can help guide conversations, mediate difficult discussions, and provide strategies for rebuilding trust.

How to Set Healthy Boundaries

Boundaries are crucial in maintaining a healthy, supportive environment for recovery. Without clear boundaries, the person in recovery may be tempted to relapse, and family members may feel overwhelmed or trapped in enabling behaviors. Healthy boundaries protect both the individual in recovery and their loved ones from emotional, physical, or psychological harm, and they allow everyone to maintain their own well-being.

What Are Boundaries?

Boundaries are the limits we establish to safeguard our physical, emotional, and mental well-being. They set the boundaries for what is considered acceptable behavior and what is not. In the context of addiction recovery, boundaries are especially important because they create structure and safety in relationships, ensuring that the person in recovery is held accountable while allowing others to protect themselves from enabling behavior or undue stress.

Types of Boundaries

1. **Physical Boundaries**: These involve personal space and physical well-being. In a recovery environment, physical boundaries may include avoiding situations where substances are present

or establishing rules about living arrangements. For example, a family member may set a boundary that they won't allow drug use in their home, or that they won't tolerate any behaviors that threaten their safety or peace of mind.

2. **Emotional Boundaries**: Emotional boundaries help to protect a person's feelings and emotional health. For example, family members may need to establish limits on the amount of emotional energy they are willing to invest in a loved one's recovery. If a person in recovery is manipulative or emotionally abusive, family members need to set boundaries to protect themselves from emotional harm.

3. **Behavioral Boundaries**: These boundaries deal with the actions and behaviors that are acceptable. For instance, a family member may set a boundary that they will no longer make excuses for a person in recovery when they fail to follow through on commitments. If the addicted person refuses to take responsibility for their actions, this boundary

helps ensure that they face the natural consequences of their behavior.

How to Set Healthy Boundaries

1. **Communicate Clearly and Assertively**: Setting boundaries involves expressing them clearly and assertively. For example, "I'm not willing to lend you money if I know you are going to use it to buy drugs." Boundaries should be communicated without guilt or anger, but rather with calm and confidence. It's important to explain the reasoning behind the boundary, making it clear that it's for the well-being of both parties.

2. **Stay Consistent**: It's not enough to set boundaries once and forget about them. They must be enforced consistently, and everyone in the household or relationship must agree to uphold them. Consistency helps to establish respect and prevents confusion or manipulation.

3. **Be Prepared for Pushback**: When boundaries are set, there may be resistance, particularly from the person in recovery. They may try to manipulate, guilt-trip, or test the limits. It's important to stand firm in the face of pushback, understanding that this is a normal part of the process. The individual in recovery may not like the boundaries, but they need to understand that these boundaries are for their own good and the good of the family.

4. **Take Care of Yourself**: Setting boundaries is not just about protecting the person in recovery—it's about protecting your own mental and emotional health. If you are a family member or loved one, you may need to take a step back, prioritize your own well-being, and ensure that your needs are being met. Boundaries can help reduce feelings of burnout and resentment that often arise when families are overextended or manipulated.

5. **Seek Professional Support**: Family therapy or individual counseling can help individuals and

families navigate the complex process of setting and maintaining boundaries. A therapist can offer strategies for enforcing boundaries in a way that fosters healthy relationships and supports the recovery process.

Communicating Effectively During Recovery

Open and honest communication is key to a successful recovery process. During recovery, emotions are often heightened, and misunderstandings can lead to conflicts or setbacks. Communication during recovery needs to be clear, compassionate, and solution-oriented, with an emphasis on mutual respect and understanding.

Key Principles for Effective Communication

1. **Listen Actively**: Active listening is an essential skill in any relationship, especially during recovery. It involves fully focusing on what the other person is saying without interrupting or formulating a response before they've finished. Active listening helps to build empathy and understanding, which is critical when emotions are running high. It's important to validate the other person's feelings, even if you don't agree with their perspective.

2. **Use "I" Statements**: Rather than saying "You always lie to me" or "You never follow through," use "I" statements that focus on your own feelings and experiences. For example, "I feel hurt when I can't trust what you say" or "I'm worried when promises are not kept." This approach avoids blaming the other person and encourages open dialogue.

3. **Stay Calm and Focused**: It's easy to get caught up in emotions during difficult conversations, but

staying calm and focused is essential for effective communication. If emotions are running high, it may be necessary to take a break and resume the conversation when both parties are calmer. Communication is most productive when both people are able to listen and speak from a place of emotional regulation.

4. **Be Honest and Transparent**: Honesty is crucial in building trust and maintaining a supportive environment. Being open about your feelings, needs, and concerns helps avoid confusion and fosters mutual respect. It's important to express need openly, whether it's the need for space, reassurance, or understanding.

5. **Avoid Criticism and Judgment**: Recovery can be fragile, and harsh criticism or judgment can feel like an attack, especially when someone is trying to make positive changes. Instead of criticizing, focus on the behavior, not the person.

6. **The Role of Family and Support Networks:**
Family members and support networks play an integral role in effective communication during recovery. They offer a listening ear, provide encouragement, and help hold the individual accountable. However, it is important that these support systems communicate their own needs and feelings as well. Mutual support and open communication are essential for both the person in recovery and their loved ones.

CHAPTER 5

SUPPORTING A LOVED ONE WITHOUT ENABLING

Helping a loved one through recovery can be one of the toughest yet most rewarding experiences. However, it's easy to slip into the trap of over helping, which can actually hinder their progress. The key to effective support is finding the balance between being there for your loved one and allowing them the space to take responsibility for their own recovery. By supporting them in a way that encourages independence while setting healthy boundaries, you can help them build the strength and confidence they need to maintain lasting sobriety.

Solving the Problem of over helping

Over helping is a common issue in families dealing with addiction, where loved ones may unintentionally take on too much responsibility for the person in recovery. The desire to help can often lead to behaviors that protect the person from facing the natural consequences of their addiction. While the intention is often out of love, over helping can enable the person's addiction to persist and prevent them from developing the necessary skills to manage their own life and recovery.

How over helping Looks:

1. **Bailing Them Out**: This includes offering financial help when they have mismanaged money due to their addiction, or constantly covering for them when they miss work or fail to meet responsibilities.

2. **Making Excuses**: When a loved one constantly deflects accountability, family

members may step in and make excuses for their behavior to others, such as explaining missed appointments or unfulfilled obligations. This prevents the person from taking responsibility for their actions.

3. **Providing a Safety Net**: Offering to house them or take care of their daily responsibilities can be helpful in certain situations, but it can also allow them to avoid confronting the realities of their behavior and becoming more self-reliant.

Why over helping Is Harmful: Over helping can create a cycle of dependency that prolongs addiction. When loved ones intervene too much, the person in recovery may not fully experience the consequences of their actions. This reduces their incentive to change, as they are shielded from the impact of their behaviors. The key in supporting someone through recovery is to strike a balance where they feel loved and encouraged, but are also held accountable for their choices.

How to stop over helping

1. **Encourage Accountability**: It's important to let your loved one experience the natural consequences of their actions, as difficult as that may be. For example, if they miss an important meeting or relapse, instead of rushing in to fix the situation, allow them to face the consequences. This can help them understand the gravity of their actions and motivate them to change.

2. **Empower, Don't Enable**: Support your loved one by encouraging them to take steps toward independence. Help them find solutions to problems, but let them do the work. For instance, if they need to find a job, assist them in looking for opportunities but allow them to handle the applications and interviews. This enables them to take charge of their life and move forward in their healing process.

3. **Set Boundaries**: Setting clear boundaries about what you will and won't do for them is crucial. For example, you can decide that you will not lend money if it's being misused, but you can offer emotional support or encouragement. By doing so, you reinforce the importance of self-sufficiency and accountability.

Encouraging Independence in Recovery

A key part of supporting a loved one without enabling is helping them build independence. Recovery is ultimately about empowering the individual to take control of their own life, and this cannot happen if they are constantly relying on others to manage their day-to-day responsibilities. Encouraging independence is about teaching the person in recovery that they have the strength and capacity to live a fulfilling life on their own terms.

Why Independence is Critical in Recovery

1. **Self-Efficacy**: The more a person in recovery is able to make decisions for themselves and see the positive results of those decisions, the more confident and capable they will feel. Independence helps build self-efficacy—the belief that they can manage their own life without resorting to substances.

2. **Preventing Relapse**: Many people relapse because they fail to develop healthy coping strategies or because they continue to depend on others for support. By encouraging independence, you help them learn how to deal with stress, triggers, and emotions without resorting to substances.

3. **Restoring Dignity**: Addiction can make individuals feel powerless and ashamed. Encouraging independence helps restore their dignity by allowing them to reclaim control over their choices and actions.

Ways to Encourage Independence

1. **Set Clear Expectations and Responsibilities**: Help your loved one take responsibility for their recovery by establishing clear expectations and tasks they need to accomplish. These could be as simple as attending therapy sessions, following a recovery plan, or managing their own finances. These responsibilities promote a sense of accomplishment and self-worth.

2. **Encourage Problem-Solving**: Rather than solving every problem for them, encourage them to come up with solutions on their own. If they are struggling with a particular issue, such as finding a job or dealing with a personal problem, encourage them to think through their options and decide what they consider this to be the most sensible and strategic choice.

3. **Support Healthy Activities**: Encourage participation in activities that foster independence

and self-reliance. Whether it's a hobby, volunteering, exercise, or a work-related goal, these activities help build confidence and self-sufficiency. Encourage them to take ownership of their recovery and make decisions that promote long-term well-being.

4. **Reinforce Successes**: Celebrate their progress, no matter how small. Reinforcing achievements, like staying sober for a certain period or managing a difficult situation without relapsing, fosters a sense of pride and reinforces the idea that they can handle challenges on their own.

Knowing When to Let Go and When to Take Charge

Knowing when to step back and when to step in is a difficult balancing act that requires patience, wisdom, and discernment. While your role as a supportive loved one is essential, there are moments when stepping back allows the person in recovery to learn and grow. On the other hand, there are situations where stepping in is necessary to ensure safety or provide critical support.

When to Step Back

1. **When They Are Facing Consequences**: If your loved one is facing the consequences of their actions—whether it's a missed appointment, a consequence at work, or the natural fallout from addiction—stepping back and allowing them to experience these consequences can be an important part of their learning process. This is not about abandoning them, but rather about giving them the space to deal with challenges on their own.

2. **When They Are Taking Responsibility**: If they are stepping up and taking responsibility for their recovery, it's important to allow them the space to continue doing so. Constantly stepping in and taking over can undermine their efforts and

prevent them from building confidence in their ability to manage their life.

3. **When They Are Developing Coping Strategies**: If your loved one is in therapy or working with a counselor to develop coping strategies for managing stress and triggers, stepping back gives them the opportunity to apply these strategies. It's important to give them the chance to experiment with new ways of thinking and acting in the real world.

When to Step In

1. **When There Is a Risk to Their Safety**: If your loved one is in a dangerous situation, such as relapse risk or self-harm, it's essential to step in and ensure their safety. You may need to intervene to prevent harm, offer support, or help them access professional assistance.

2. **When They Are in Crisis**: If your loved one is experiencing a crisis, such as a mental health breakdown, physical health issues, or severe emotional distress, stepping in is necessary. Offering immediate help, emotional support, and directing them to professional resources can make a critical difference in their recovery.

3. **When They Ask for Help**: Sometimes, the best way to support a loved one is simply to be there when they ask for help. If they are struggling with a specific issue, like an overwhelming emotional challenge, helping them work through it—while still encouraging their independence—can be a valuable form of support.

4. **When They Are Not Meeting Their Commitments**: If your loved one is not following through on important recovery tasks, such as attending therapy, staying sober, or fulfilling work or personal responsibilities, it may be necessary to

step in to provide guidance and support. This can help reinforce the seriousness of their commitments and prevent relapse.

CHAPTER 6

PROMOTING ACCOUNTABILITY AND RESPONSIBILITY

Recovery from addiction is not a passive process. It requires active participation from the individual in recovery and consistent support from their loved ones. One of the key elements of successful recovery is accountability—the ability of the person in recovery to take ownership of their actions and decisions. This fosters responsibility, which is essential for long-term sobriety and personal growth. As a loved one, your role is to encourage and support this process without enabling or doing the work for them. Creating an environment of structure, consistency, and accountability within the family can significantly contribute to the person's recovery journey.

How to Encourage Your Loved One to Take Ownership of Their Recovery

Taking ownership of one's recovery means actively engaging in the process, making decisions that align with sobriety, and understanding the impact of their actions. Encouraging this sense of responsibility can be difficult, especially when the individual has been in denial or has relied on others to manage their behaviors. However, promoting accountability is crucial for their growth and success in recovery.

Why Ownership Is Important

1. **Self-Empowerment**: When someone in recovery takes ownership of their recovery, they are empowering themselves to make decisions, solve problems, and control their own destiny. This helps reduce feelings of helplessness or

victimization, which can often accompany addiction.

2. **A Sense of Purpose:** Taking Ownership Fuels Clarity and Direction. The individual is no longer relying on others to determine their path. Instead, they are motivated by their own goals, whether that's staying sober, repairing relationships, or building a new life.

3. **Prevention of Relapse**: When someone owns their recovery, they are more likely to follow through with the difficult decisions that are necessary to maintain sobriety. They are less likely to rely on others to solve their problems or deflect responsibility.

Strategies to Promote Ownership

1. **Set Clear Expectations**: Clearly communicate your expectations and the importance of taking responsibility for recovery. For example, "I expect

you to attend your counseling sessions," or "It's important for you to be honest about your progress and setbacks." Be firm but compassionate, ensuring that they understand their role in the process.

2. **Encourage Goal-Setting**: Help your loved one set achievable and meaningful goals for their recovery. Encourage them to set both short-term and long-term goals, and make sure these goals are specific, measurable, and realistic. For example, a short-term goal could be attending therapy regularly, while a long-term goal might be rebuilding relationships or maintaining sobriety for a year.

3. **Encourage Self-Reflection**: Support your loved one in practicing self-reflection. Encourage them to routinely reflect on their progress, confront challenges, and understand their emotions. Self-reflection helps them recognize patterns of behavior, identify triggers, and make adjustments

as needed. Tools like journaling or mindfulness exercises can be helpful in this process.

4. **Hold Them Accountable**: It's essential to hold your loved one accountable for their actions, both positive and negative. When they fulfill their responsibilities, praise their efforts, reinforcing their positive behavior. Conversely, when they fail to meet their commitments, calmly and respectfully remind them of their responsibilities. This creates a structure of accountability, which is essential for their growth.

5. **Support Decision-Making**: Rather than solving problems for your loved one, encourage them to think through situations and make their own decisions. Offer guidance when necessary, but empower them to take responsibility for their choices. For instance, if they're facing a difficult social situation, help them weigh the pros and

cons of different actions and encourage them to choose the best course of action for their recovery.

6. **Provide Opportunities for Independent Success**: Create situations where your loved one can succeed on their own. This could be managing their finances, taking care of daily tasks, or fulfilling responsibilities without your assistance. Celebrating these successes, no matter how small, reinforces their ability to take charge of their own recovery.

Creating Structure and Consistency in Family Life

Structure and consistency in family life provide a sense of stability that can significantly enhance recovery efforts. When a person in recovery returns home or interacts with family, the environment must be conducive to sobriety, safety, and personal growth. Family dynamics and routines should be aligned with the goal of promoting responsibility and self-discipline.

George Leo

Why Structure and Consistency Matter

1. **Reduces Chaos**: Addiction often disrupts the family structure, leading to chaos, unpredictability, and instability. A consistent routine can help restore order and create a safe, reliable environment that supports recovery.

2. **Encourages Healthy Habits**: A structured environment promotes healthy routines that support sobriety, such as regular sleep, meals, exercise, and therapy. By sticking to these routines, the person in recovery can build habits that align with their recovery goals.

3. **Builds Trust**: Consistency in behavior and expectations helps rebuild trust. When everyone in the family is consistent in their actions, it reinforces a sense of reliability and dependability, which is essential in recovery.

How to Create Structure and Consistency

1. **Establish Routines**: Create daily routines that include healthy activities, such as exercise, work, therapy, and time for personal reflection. Encourage your loved one to stick to these routines, as they provide a sense of accomplishment and normalcy.

2. **Set Boundaries and Expectations**: Clearly define the family's expectations and rules regarding behavior, responsibilities, and participation in recovery. For example, you might have rules about no substance use in the house, attending therapy appointments, or curfews. Consistently enforcing these boundaries creates a stable environment for recovery.

3. **Create a Safe, Supportive Home Environment**: A home that is free of triggers, chaos, or substance use is essential for recovery. This may involve removing substances from the

home, limiting contact with negative influences, and fostering an emotionally supportive atmosphere where your loved one feels encouraged to succeed.

4. **Encourage Responsibility for Household Tasks**: One of the key aspects of promoting accountability is encouraging your loved one to contribute to the family dynamic by taking responsibility for household chores or other duties. This teaches them to be responsible for their actions and helps them feel like an active, contributing member of the family.

5. **Consistency in Communication**: Consistent, open communication is essential in maintaining a stable family environment. Regularly check in with your loved one about their progress, challenges, and feelings. Be honest, clear, and respectful in your communication, and encourage the same openness from them.

Solving the Challenge of Relapse Management

Relapse is a common and often painful part of addiction recovery. It doesn't mean failure—it's a part of the process that requires understanding, patience, and a solution-oriented approach. When relapse occurs, it can be a difficult and emotional experience for everyone involved. The key is how to respond to it—what steps to take to prevent further setbacks and how to help your loved one get back on track.

Why Relapse Happens

1. **Triggers and Temptations**: Stress, emotional pain, or exposure to substance use can trigger a relapse. People in recovery may face situations that tempt them to return to old habits, especially if they haven't fully developed the coping strategies needed to handle those triggers.

2. **Lack of Support**: Recovery is often more difficult without a solid support system. If a person in

recovery feels isolated or unsupported, they may struggle to maintain sobriety.

3. **Unrealistic Expectations**: Sometimes, individuals in recovery may set unrealistic expectations for themselves, thinking they should be able to stay sober without experiencing any setbacks. This can lead to feelings of shame or defeat when they do relapse, which only exacerbates the issue.

How to Manage Relapse

1. **Acknowledge It Without Judgment**: If your loved one relapses, the first step is to acknowledge the relapse without shame or judgment. While it's important to address the consequences of relapse, approaching the situation with compassion and understanding will help your loved one feel supported, not blamed.

2. **Assess What Led to the Relapse**: Try to understand the underlying causes of the relapse. Was it due to stress, exposure to a trigger, or

emotional distress? Work together to identify patterns that may have contributed to the relapse. This insight can help both you and your loved one plan for future challenges.

3. **Reaffirm the Commitment to Recovery**: Encourage your loved one to reaffirm their commitment to recovery. A relapse does not erase the progress they've made, and it's important for them to understand that they can still move forward. Help them see that setbacks are part of the process and that it's possible to learn from mistakes.

4. **Encourage Reengagement with Recovery Resources**: After a relapse, it's important for your loved one to return to their recovery program as soon as possible. This could mean attending therapy, support groups, or sober living programs. Encourage them to seek help and re-engage with their recovery tools and support network.

5. **Develop a Plan for Relapse Prevention**: Work together to develop a relapse prevention plan. This plan should include coping strategies for managing stress, avoiding triggers, and seeking support when needed. Having a plan in place gives your loved one concrete steps to follow when faced with challenges, which increases the chances of long-term sobriety.

6. **Reaffirm Your Support**: Remind your loved one that your support is unwavering, and that you are there to help them get back on track. Reaffirming your belief in their ability to recover and your willingness to help them through challenges is critical to maintaining their motivation.

PART 3: HEALING THE FAMILY UNIT

CHAPTER 7

ADDRESSING FAMILY TRAUMA CAUSED BY ADDICTION

Addiction causes a ripple effect throughout the family, often leaving deep emotional scars. While the individual struggling with addiction may be the focal point, those close to them, particularly spouses, children, and parents, also experience trauma. Unresolved pain, grief, anger, and disappointment can become entrenched in family dynamics, making it difficult to heal and move forward. The process of healing requires confronting and processing these emotions while working toward **forgiveness**, understanding, and reconnection.

George Leo

Solving the Problem of Unresolved Pain

Unresolved pain is one of the most significant barriers to family healing. Years of emotional neglect, betrayal, and unfulfilled promises can lead to deep-seated hurt. For the person who has struggled with addiction, they may have caused harm to their loved ones by lying, breaking trust, or neglecting family responsibilities. For the family members, the hurt can feel overwhelming, as they may have felt betrayed, unsupported, or abandoned.

The Impact of Unresolved Pain

1. **Emotional Distance**: Unresolved pain creates emotional distance between family members. This distance can manifest as anger, silence, or avoidance. While these behaviors may seem protective, they prevent families from addressing the core issues that need healing.

2. **Disrupted Communication**: Pain often leads to breakdowns in communication. Family members

may find it difficult to express their feelings without triggering defensive responses or guilt from the individual in recovery. This makes honest conversations about the past difficult and prevents healing.

3. **Resentment**: Unresolved pain can lead to lingering resentment, which undermines trust and makes it difficult for family members to move forward together. If left unchecked, resentment can poison the entire family dynamic.

How to Resolve Unresolved Pain

1. **Open and Honest Communication**: Healing begins with the ability to talk openly about the hurt. While these conversations may be painful, they are necessary for acknowledging the past and starting the process of rebuilding. Family members must create a safe space where everyone feels heard, validated, and respected.

2. **Allow for Emotional Expression**: Encourage family members to express their emotions, whether it's grief, anger, or disappointment. It's important that everyone feels safe enough to voice their feelings without fear of judgment or retaliation. This allows everyone to release the pent-up emotions that may have been festering for years.

3. **Seek Professional Guidance**: Family therapy can be a helpful tool for processing unresolved pain. A therapist can guide the family through difficult conversations, help individuals express their feelings constructively, and provide strategies for healing. Individual therapy for family members may also be necessary to process personal trauma and pain.

4. **Acknowledge the Hurt**: The person who was struggling with addiction must acknowledge the pain they caused and take responsibility for their actions. This requires humility and accountability.

Without acknowledgment, it's difficult for family members to begin the healing process.

Tools for Processing Grief, Anger, and Disappointment

Grief, anger, and disappointment are natural responses to addiction and its impact on the family. Each of these emotions is valid and needs to be addressed in order for healing to take place. Processing these emotions requires patience, self-compassion, and a willingness to face painful memories.

Ways to Process Grief, Anger, and Disappointment

1. Grief

- **Acknowledge the Losses**: Addiction often results in a series of losses—emotional, financial, and relational. Family members may grieve the loss of trust, the loss of safety, or the loss of the relationship they once had with the individual struggling with addiction. Acknowledging these losses and mourning them is essential for healing.

- **Create Rituals of Remembrance**: Family members may find it helpful to create rituals that honor what has been lost. Whether it's writing letters, holding a family gathering, or planting a tree, these rituals provide a meaningful way to process grief and acknowledge the past.

2. **Anger**

- **Express Anger Constructively**: Anger, while natural, can become destructive if not managed properly. Encourage family members to express anger in healthy ways, such as journaling, exercising, or having calm discussions where feelings are expressed without aggression or blame.

- **Understand the Source of Anger**: Often, anger is rooted in feelings of betrayal, fear, or helplessness. By understanding the source of anger, family members can begin to release it and move toward forgiveness.

3. Disappointment

- **Reframe Expectations**: Addiction often leads to unmet expectations, and family members may feel deeply disappointed by promises that were broken. Reframing expectations can help reduce disappointment by recognizing that recovery is a process, and that setbacks are part of the journey.

Practice Self-Compassion: It's important for family members to be compassionate toward themselves as they process disappointment. Recovery requires patience, and occasional challenges are part of the process. Self-compassion allows family members to continue to move forward without feeling guilty or discouraged.

How to Move Forward Together

Moving forward together requires the family to come to terms with the past while creating a new, healthier future. This is not about forgetting the pain, but rather finding ways to rebuild trust, strengthen relationships, and support one another in the journey toward healing.

Steps to Move Forward

1. **Commit to Healing**: Every family member must be committed to healing, both individually and collectively. This may mean attending therapy, engaging in open conversations, or practicing forgiveness. Commitment to the process creates the foundation for rebuilding the family unit.

2. **Create New Traditions**: Building new, positive traditions can help replace the negative patterns of the past. Whether it's shared activities, family rituals, or simple moments of connection, these new traditions foster a sense of unity and help the family bond in healthy ways.

CHAPTER 8

REBUILDING TRUST AND CONNECTION

Addiction often shatters trust, and restoring it becomes one of the toughest hurdles in the recovery process. Addiction has likely caused betrayal, broken promises, and actions that have undermined the foundation of the family's relationships. Restoring trust takes time, understanding, and the courage to be open and honest.

However, with commitment and effort from all family members, it's possible to restore trust and emotional connection.

Solving the Problem of Mistrust after Addiction

Mistrust is a natural response when someone has repeatedly hurt or disappointed those they love. It can take many forms—fear that the person will relapse, anxiety about their promises being broken again, or doubt about their ability to change. The challenge is overcoming this mistrust while allowing space for healing.

Why Mistrust Happens

1. **Betrayal of Trust**: Addiction often involves deception, lying, and broken promises. Family members may feel that trust has been irreparably damaged.

2. **Fear of Relapse**: There is often a lingering fear that the person in recovery will relapse, leading to further disappointment and hurt.

3. **Resentment and Disappointment**: Even when a loved one is in recovery, family members may

harbor resentment or disappointment from the past, making it hard to move past the hurt.

How to Rebuild Trust

Rebuilding trust: It demands reliability and honesty in every action. To truly embrace sobriety, a person in recovery must back their intentions with consistent actions rather than relying solely on words. This might include regular attendance at recovery meetings, being open about their struggles, and keeping promises.

1. **Apologize and Make Amends**: The person in recovery must take full responsibility for their actions and apologize without justification or excuses. Making amends is a necessary part of rebuilding trust. This doesn't mean that everything can be fixed overnight, but it's an essential step toward healing.

2. **Reassure Family Members**: Rebuilding trust also involves reassuring family members that recovery is the priority. This might include being available for difficult conversations, checking in regularly, or seeking professional help to navigate difficult emotions.

3. **Patience and Time**: Trust doesn't return overnight. It requires time and patience. Family members must allow themselves to be vulnerable, but they must also give the person in recovery time to prove that they can be trusted again.

How to Reconnect Emotionally with Your Loved One

Emotional reconnection is vital to healing. Addiction creates emotional distance, and rebuilding this connection takes time and effort from both sides.

Steps to Reconnect Emotionally

Spend Quality Time Together: Reconnecting emotionally requires spending time together in a healthy, supportive environment. This could mean doing activities you both enjoy or simply talking without distractions. The aim is to create new shared experiences that strengthen connection and closeness.

1. **Practice Empathy**: Understand that both parties have been through a lot. Practice empathy for each other's struggles and pain. When family members can step into each other's shoes and acknowledge the emotional toll addiction has taken, it fosters connection and understanding.

2. **Be Vulnerable**: Both sides must be willing to be emotionally vulnerable in order to reconnect. This might mean sharing fears, disappointments, or hopes for the future. Being open and vulnerable

strengthens trust and deepens emotional connections.

Strengthening Family Relationships Through Forgiveness

Forgiveness is a powerful tool in the healing process for families affected by addiction. Addiction causes a cascade of emotional wounds, broken promises, and deep disappointments. Over time, these hurts can create walls between family members, making it difficult to rebuild relationships and move forward together. However, without forgiveness, these walls may remain, hindering the possibility of emotional reconnection and healing.

Forgiveness doesn't mean erasing the past or justifying hurtful actions. Rather, it is about letting go of the desire for retribution, releasing negative emotions like anger and resentment, and choosing to move forward in a healthier, more compassionate way. In the context of addiction recovery, forgiveness helps families create a new chapter—one where the past doesn't define the future, and where emotional healing can take root.

Why Forgiveness Is Essential in Healing

1. **Releases Resentment**: Holding onto anger and resentment toward a loved one can be emotionally and physically draining. Resentment often festers and becomes toxic, preventing individuals from healing and growing. Forgiveness allows family members to release these negative emotions, which can free them to move forward.

2. **Restores Emotional Health**: Un-forgiveness can lead to stress, anxiety, and depression, especially for those who have been hurt. It can negatively impact one's emotional and even physical well-being. When forgiveness is embraced, it promotes emotional health, reduces anxiety, and allows for the restoration of emotional balance.

3. **Restores Hope and Trust**: Addiction often erodes trust, and forgiveness is the first step toward restoring it. While trust may take time to rebuild, the act of forgiveness signals a willingness to move past the pain and open the door to a renewed relationship. Forgiveness gives the family hope for the future and the possibility of a stronger, more connected relationship.

4. **Promotes Mutual Healing**: Forgiveness isn't just for the person who has been hurt—it also facilitates healing for the person who has caused the harm. The individual in recovery may feel weighed down by guilt and shame, and forgiveness offers them a path to emotional release. It signals that they are accepted, and it can motivate them to continue on their path of recovery.

5. **Fosters Compassion and Understanding**: Forgiveness allows family members to develop a deeper understanding of the challenges the person in recovery faces. It fosters empathy and compassion, allowing family members to view the

situation through their loved one's eyes. This shared understanding can build a more supportive and nurturing space for recovery.

CHAPTER 9

FOSTERING RESILIENCE IN CHILDREN AFFECTED BY ADDICTION

Children are often the silent victims of addiction, impacted by the behaviors and emotional struggles of their parents or caregivers. The effects of substance abuse on children are profound and can shape their mental, emotional, and social development in ways that last long into adulthood. However, fostering resilience in children affected by addiction is possible. By providing support, teaching healthy coping mechanisms, and building a strong support system, families can help these children develop the emotional strength they need to overcome the challenges they face and thrive despite their circumstances.

Solving the Impact of Substance Abuse on Children

Children who grow up in environments affected by addiction are at increased risk of developing a wide range of emotional and psychological issues. The impacts of substance abuse on children can include neglect, trauma, confusion, and a sense of insecurity. These children often experience inconsistent care, emotional withdrawal, and may even witness or experience abuse.

Key Impacts of Substance Abuse on Children:

1. **Emotional Instability**: Children of parents with addiction may experience a range of emotional responses, from confusion and sadness to anger and frustration. They may struggle to understand

why their parent behaves the way they do or why the family environment is unstable.

2. **Fear and Anxiety**: The unpredictable nature of a household affected by addiction can cause children to live in constant fear. They may worry about their parent's health, safety, or behavior. This anxiety can affect their social interactions and academic performance.

3. **Neglect and Emotional Absence**: A parent's addiction may cause them to be emotionally or physically absent, leaving children feeling neglected. Without proper care and attention, children may develop feelings of unworthiness or abandonment.

4. **Behavioral Problems**: In some cases, children may imitate the coping mechanisms of their addicted parents, which can include aggressive behavior, poor decision-making, or substance misuse themselves.

How to Address the Impact:

1. **Ensure Emotional Security**: The most important step in mitigating the impact of substance abuse on children is ensuring that they feel safe and loved. This means providing a stable home environment, with clear boundaries, reliable routines, and a nurturing atmosphere.

2. **Open Conversations**: Children need to be given age-appropriate explanations about addiction. When parents or caregivers talk openly about the issue, it helps children understand what is happening and reduces the sense of shame or confusion they might feel.

3. **Limit Exposure to Chaos**: Shield children from witnessing drug use, fights, or neglectful behavior. The more a child is exposed to the chaotic aspects of addiction, the more likely they are to experience trauma and emotional distress.

4. **Provide Therapy and Counseling**: Counseling can help children process the confusion, fear, and

pain they experience. Therapy can teach children how to express their emotions, work through their feelings, and build healthy coping strategies.

Teaching Healthy Coping Mechanisms

The children of addicts often struggle with managing their own emotions, as they have not been taught how to process their feelings in a healthy way. In order to foster resilience, it is crucial to teach these children healthy coping mechanisms that they can use when faced with challenges, stress, or emotional turmoil.

Healthy Coping Mechanisms to Teach Children:

1. **Emotional Expression**: Encourage children to express their emotions in healthy ways, such as talking about their feelings, drawing, journaling, or engaging in physical activities. Emotional expression is key to preventing the suppression of

feelings, which can lead to long-term psychological issues.

2. **Mindfulness and Relaxation**: Techniques such as deep breathing, mindfulness, or guided relaxation exercises can help children manage anxiety and stress. Teaching children to slow down and focus on the present moment can help them gain control over overwhelming emotions.

3. **Problem-Solving Skills**: Children need to learn how to approach challenges with a problem-solving mindset. Encourage them to look at difficulties as opportunities for growth and to brainstorm potential solutions. This builds resilience and confidence.

4. **Self-Soothing**: Help children develop self-soothing techniques, like listening to calming music, taking walks, or engaging in hobbies that make them feel good. These techniques can help

them feel more in control of their emotions in tough situations.

5. **Positive Self-Talk**: Teach children to replace negative self-talk with positive affirmations. Children who have grown up in a household affected by addiction may internalize feelings of guilt, inadequacy, or anger. Positive self-talk can help counteract these destructive thoughts and build their self-esteem.

Building a Support System for Children

In addition to teaching coping skills, it's critical that children affected by addiction have access to a strong support system. This includes both family members who are committed to their well-being and external support networks, such as trusted adults, counselors, or community programs.

Building a Robust Support System:

1. **Extended Family Support**: In cases where the immediate family is struggling with addiction,

extended family members (such as grandparents, aunts, or uncles) can play an important role in providing stability. Having someone to turn to for emotional support can help mitigate the effects of addiction at home.

2. **Mentors and Role Models**: Positive role models are incredibly important for children who are dealing with the effects of addiction. Mentors—whether through school, sports, or community groups—can provide guidance, encouragement, and emotional support.

3. **Peer Support**: Connecting with peers who understand what they are going through can be healing for children. Support groups specifically designed for children of addicted parents offer a space for shared experiences, validation, and peer-led emotional support.

4. **Therapists and Counselors**: Mental health professionals can help children process their

emotions and develop resilience. A counselor can provide children with coping tools, teach emotional regulation, and offer a safe space for expression.

5. **Community Resources**: Many communities have programs for children affected by addiction, such as youth groups, after-school programs, and extracurricular activities. These programs can give children a sense of normalcy and a way to build social connections outside of the addiction dynamics at home.

Fostering resilience in children is an ongoing process. It requires creating an environment where children feel emotionally safe, valued, and empowered. It involves teaching them healthy ways to cope with stress, building their self-esteem, and ensuring that they have a network of supportive individuals who are invested in their growth and well-being.

PART 4: PRACTICAL STRATEGIES FOR LONG-TERM RECOVERY

CHAPTER 10

CREATING A RECOVERY-FRIENDLY HOME ENVIRONMENT

A supportive and structured home environment is key to fostering long-term recovery. People in recovery need a space that minimizes triggers, provides emotional support, and encourages healthy habits. By making intentional changes to the home, families can create a nurturing space that promotes sobriety and growth.

How to Minimize Triggers at Home

Triggers—specific people, places, or activities that remind the individual of past substance use—can pose a major challenge to long-term sobriety.

Identifying and minimizing these triggers is essential to creating a safe, recovery-friendly environment.

Steps to Minimize Triggers

1. **Remove Substances from the Home**: One of the first steps in creating a recovery-friendly home is removing any substances (alcohol, drugs, paraphernalia) that may tempt or trigger the person in recovery. If certain foods, drinks, or even particular settings are triggers, consider making changes to reduce exposure to those triggers.

2. **Limit Stress and Conflict**: Stress and emotional conflict can be significant triggers for relapse. By creating a calm, stress-reduced home environment, you can help the person in recovery maintain their emotional equilibrium. Encourage open communication, conflict resolution, and a calm, supportive atmosphere.

3. **Establish Clear Boundaries**: Boundaries are important in any home, but they are particularly essential for maintaining sobriety. Setting clear rules about behavior, substance use, and expectations within the home helps the person in recovery feel supported and secure.

4. **Create Healthy Rituals and Habits**: Establish new rituals that support recovery. This might include family dinners, daily exercise, or spiritual practices like meditation or prayer. These activities can create positive associations in the home and help replace the unhealthy behaviors linked to addiction.

Solving the Challenge of Maintaining a Sober Lifestyle

Maintaining a sober lifestyle requires consistent effort and support. For those in recovery, temptations and challenges will arise. The family plays an essential role in supporting their loved one's commitment to sobriety, but the individual in recovery must also develop personal strategies for maintaining their sobriety.

Practical Strategies for Maintaining Sobriety:

1. **Stay Connected to Support Networks**: Regular participation in support groups such as AA (Alcoholics Anonymous) or NA (Narcotics Anonymous) provides a structured way for individuals in recovery to stay connected to others who understand their journey. These groups offer accountability and emotional support.

2. **Develop Healthy Routines**: Creating new routines that prioritize health and well-being is essential. This can include daily self-care practices like exercise, cooking healthy meals, engaging in hobbies, and getting adequate rest. These positive routines help establish a life of purpose and stability.

3. **Work through Emotional Challenges**: Recovery isn't just about stopping substance use; it's also about addressing the emotional and psychological issues that led to the addiction in the first place. Therapy, journaling, and mindfulness practices.

CHAPTER 11

NAVIGATING RELAPSE TOGETHER

Relapse is a common and challenging part of the recovery process. For families, it can feel like a painful setback, but it's essential to approach relapse with understanding and compassion. The journey to sobriety is rarely linear, and setbacks—while disheartening—are not failures. In fact, they can provide valuable lessons that help to strengthen long-term recovery. It's important to navigate relapse together as a family, addressing it without judgment, creating a clear response plan, and learning from setbacks to continue the path of healing and recovery.

How to Solve the Problem of Relapse Without Judgment

One of the most common reactions to relapse is judgment. Family members may feel betrayed, angry, or discouraged when their loved one relapses. These feelings are valid but can be harmful to the person in recovery, reinforcing feelings of shame and guilt that can further hinder progress.

To effectively navigate relapse, it's important to shift the focus from blame to support. Recovery is a difficult process, and setbacks are often part of it. Instead of viewing relapse as a failure, see it as a challenge to be worked through together.

Key Steps to Solve Relapse Without Judgment

1. **Avoid Shame and Blame**: Rather than focusing on the negative aspects of relapse, aim to offer support. Reassure your loved one that you understand how difficult recovery is and that setbacks don't define their ability to recover. Acknowledge the courage it takes to get back on track after a relapse.

2. **Understand the Triggers**: Relapse is often caused by specific triggers—stress, emotions, people, or places that are linked to substance use. It's important to work with your loved one to identify these triggers, as this can help prevent future relapses.

3. **Keep Communication Open**: When relapse occurs, the lines of communication should remain open. Avoiding confrontation or expressing anger will only push the person in recovery further away. Instead, express concern and love, and discuss what led to the relapse in a constructive and empathetic way.

4. **Reaffirm Commitment to Recovery**: Reassure your loved one that relapse does not negate all the progress they've made. Acknowledge the work they've done and reaffirm your support for their recovery. It's important to remind them that

recovery is a process, and this setback is just a part of that.

Creating a Relapse Response Plan

A relapse response plan is a proactive way to handle relapse if it occurs. This plan should include specific steps for both the person in recovery and the family, ensuring that everyone knows how to respond effectively, safely, and without judgment.

Steps to Create a Relapse Response Plan:

1. **Establish Clear Boundaries and Expectations**: Everyone in the family needs to understand their role in the response plan. Establishing clear boundaries—such as where the individual can or cannot go, who they can or cannot associate with, and what behaviors are unacceptable—can help prevent relapse and ensure the person in recovery is supported.

2. **Set up Immediate Support**: When relapse occurs, it's important to have a support system in

place. This may include calling a sponsor, reaching out to a therapist, or attending a recovery meeting immediately. Having an action plan helps the person in recovery feel supported rather than isolated or judged.

3. **Assess the Trigger and the Circumstances**: When relapse happens, take time to assess what triggered it. Was it a specific event, emotional distress, or external pressures? Understanding the cause of the relapse will provide insight into how to avoid similar triggers in the future.

4. **Provide Emotional Support, Not Ultimatums**: Rather than offering ultimatums or threats, provide emotional support and understanding. Reaffirm your commitment to helping them stay sober and encourage them to take the necessary steps to return to recovery. Setbacks should not be viewed as a complete failure, but as a learning experience that strengthens resolve.

5. **Revisit Recovery Goals**: A relapse may signal that certain aspects of the recovery process need to be reassessed. Together, with the guidance of a therapist or recovery coach, review the goals and adjust the recovery plan as necessary. This could mean increasing therapy sessions, re-engaging with support groups, or creating new strategies for managing stress.

Learning from Setbacks to Strengthen Recovery

Relapse is a powerful reminder that addiction is a chronic illness that requires lifelong management. While relapse can feel discouraging, it's also an opportunity to learn and adjust the recovery plan to make it more sustainable in the long term.

How to Learn from Setbacks

1. **Reflect on the Relapse**: Take time to reflect on what led to the relapse. Was it a particular emotional trigger? A stressful situation? A lack of support? This reflection can provide important

insights into areas of the recovery process that need strengthening or modification.

2. **Develop New Coping Strategies**: If certain situations or emotions were a trigger for the relapse, work together to develop new coping strategies. This might involve deepening mindfulness practices, engaging in new forms of therapy, or finding new ways to handle stress.

3. **Strengthen Support Systems**: One of the key lessons learned from relapse is the importance of support. Revisit your loved one's support system and look for ways to enhance it. This could involve increasing attendance at support group meetings, finding new mentors, or exploring additional recovery resources.

4. **Reaffirm Commitment to Sobriety**: After a relapse, it's important for the person in recovery to reaffirm their commitment to sobriety. Discuss how recovery fits into the bigger picture of their

life and the goals they have for their future. This reaffirms their motivation and reinforces the importance of the recovery process.

5. **Don't Let Relapse Define You:** Recovery is about progress, not perfection. Encourage your loved one to see relapse as just another challenge to overcome, not a defining moment. By viewing setbacks as opportunities for growth, rather than defeat, the road to lasting sobriety becomes a series of steps forward rather than a destination to reach.

CHAPTER 12

FINDING AND USING OUTSIDE RESOURCES

Addiction recovery is not something that can be achieved in isolation. It's important to utilize a variety of external resources, from professional help to community and peer support, in order to create a comprehensive support system. These resources provide essential tools, encouragement, and accountability during the recovery process. For families, seeking outside resources can help reduce isolation, provide expert guidance, and connect with others who understand the experience of addiction and recovery.

How to Solve the Isolation That Families Often Face

When addiction is present in a family, it can create a

deep sense of isolation. Family members often feel alone, without a clear understanding of how to support their loved one or how to deal with the stress of addiction. This isolation can be exacerbated by shame, secrecy, or lack of information.

How to Overcome Isolation:

1. **Join Support Groups**: Family members should consider joining groups like Al-Anon (for families of alcoholics) or Nar-Anon (for families of drug addicts). These groups provide a space where families can share their experiences, learn from others, and gain emotional support. Knowing that others are going through similar challenges can help break the sense of isolation.

2. **Seek Counseling**: Family therapy can be an important resource for healing. Professional counselors can help families navigate the complex emotions and dynamics that arise from living with addiction. Therapy can also help family members

learn how to communicate more effectively and support each other.

3. **Educate Yourself About Addiction**: Understanding addiction is key to reducing feelings of isolation. Families who educate themselves about the nature of addiction, recovery processes, and the challenges involved are better equipped to cope with the realities of living with addiction. There are many resources available online, in books, and through support groups that offer education and guidance.

4. **Strengthen Social Connections**: In addition to formal support groups, it's important for family members to cultivate relationships outside of the addiction dynamic. This might mean reconnecting with friends, joining community groups, or participating in activities that provide emotional and social support.

The Role of Support Groups Like Al-Anon and Nar-Anon

Support groups like Al-Anon and Nar-Anon offer a unique opportunity for families affected by addiction to come together, share experiences, and find solace. These groups are not just for those in recovery, but for family members and friends who are looking for guidance, connection, and emotional support.

Benefits of Support Groups:

1. **Emotional Support**: Support groups offer a safe space for family members to express their emotions, knowing that they are surrounded by others who truly understand their struggles. This emotional connection can be incredibly healing and help families feel less alone.

2. **Practical Guidance**: In addition to emotional support, these groups offer practical advice on how to cope with the challenges of living with addiction. They can help family members set

boundaries, communicate more effectively, and provide strategies for self-care.

3. **A Sense of Community**: By attending support groups, family members can build relationships with others in similar situations. This sense of community can help reduce feelings of isolation and provide a network of support when the going gets tough.

Using Community and Professional Resources for Help

In addition to support groups, there are a variety of community and professional resources that can help families and individuals in recovery. These might include therapy, addiction treatment centers, educational programs, and online resources.

Professional Resources

Therapists and Counselors: Working with a therapist who specializes in addiction and family dynamics can be invaluable in the recovery process. Family therapy helps to rebuild trust, improve communication, and address the emotional wounds caused by addiction.

Addiction Treatment Centers: If the person in recovery is struggling to maintain sobriety, addiction treatment centers.

CHAPTER 13

FOCUSING ON SELF-CARE FOR FAMILY MEMBERS

Living with a loved one who is struggling with addiction is incredibly demanding, and it can often feel like the needs of the person in recovery overshadow the well-being of the family members who are supporting them. However, in order to be an effective source of help and strength for someone in recovery, family members must prioritize their own health and well-being. Self-care is not a luxury—it is a necessity that enables family members to stay emotionally and physically resilient, ensuring they are able to provide ongoing support without burning out.

Solving the Neglect of Your Own Well-Being

When a family member is in active addiction or recovery, it's easy for those supporting them to lose sight of their own needs. This can happen gradually as family members become consumed by the demands of caregiving, or by their own emotional responses to the situation. Over time, neglecting self-care can lead to exhaustion, frustration, and burnout.

Why Self-Care Matters

1. **Emotional Exhaustion**: Constantly focusing on someone else's needs while ignoring your own can lead to emotional depletion. This can result in feelings of resentment, anger, or helplessness, which only complicate the healing process for both the individual in recovery and their family.

2. **Physical Health**: Stress from dealing with addiction can have a serious impact on physical health. The constant worry, lack of sleep, and emotional strain can weaken the immune system, cause physical fatigue, and increase the risk of chronic conditions such as heart disease, depression, or anxiety.

3. **Burnout**: Without self-care, family members can experience burnout—where they feel emotionally drained and mentally overwhelmed. This can reduce their ability to effectively support their loved one or even maintain their own quality of life.

How to Prioritize Self-Care

1. **Set Boundaries**: Establishing clear, healthy boundaries is a vital part of practicing self-care. Family members must learn to say no when necessary, protect their own emotional space, and refuse to take on responsibilities that are not theirs to carry.

2. **Make Time for Yourself**: Carve out time each day for activities that replenish your energy. Whether it's exercising, reading, engaging in a hobby, or spending time with friends, making time

for yourself allows you to recharge and maintain balance in your life.

3. **Seek Support**: Don't try to handle the challenges of addiction and recovery on your own. It's important to seek out support from friends, family members, or professional counselors. Having a reliable support system can help you cope with stress and provide a safe space for expressing your feelings.

4. **Practice Mindfulness**: Mindfulness practices such as meditation, deep breathing, or journaling can help manage stress and increase emotional resilience. Taking a few minutes each day to clear your mind and focus on the present can help reduce anxiety and improve overall well-being.

Building Your Own Emotional and Physical Resilience

In the face of the stress and emotional toll that comes with addiction and recovery, it's essential for family members to build both emotional and physical resilience. Resilience is the strength to recover from challenges, adapt to adversity, and maintain your best performance even in tough situations.

Building Emotional Resilience

Embrace Your Emotions: Emotional resilience begins with acknowledging your own feelings. It's important to allow yourself to feel anger, sadness, or frustration without judgment. Holding back emotions can contribute to overwhelming stress and the risk of burnout. Practice self-compassion by recognizing that your emotions are valid and part of the healing process.

1. **Develop Coping Strategies**: Resilient family members develop healthy coping strategies to deal with stress and negative emotions. These can include talking to a trusted friend, engaging in physical activities, or practicing relaxation techniques. Find healthy ways to process and release emotional tension.

2. **Stay Optimistic**: Emotional resilience is often tied to maintaining a hopeful perspective. This doesn't mean ignoring the challenges of addiction or recovery, but it does mean choosing to focus on progress, however small, and staying hopeful about the possibility of positive change.

3. **Learn to Accept Uncertainty**: Recovery is unpredictable, and outcomes are not always immediate. Developing emotional resilience means learning to live with uncertainty and trusting that progress will happen in its own time. Cultivate patience and give yourself permission to take things one day at a time.

Building Physical Resilience

1. **Exercise Regularly**: Physical activity is one of the best ways to reduce stress and increase energy. Whether it's going for a walk, taking yoga classes, or engaging in more vigorous exercise, movement helps release built-up tension, boost mood, and improve overall health.

2. **Eat Well**: A balanced diet that includes nutrient-rich foods plays a significant role in both physical and emotional health. Eating regular, wholesome meals helps stabilize energy levels, reduces stress, and enhances the body's ability to cope with physical demands.

3. **Sleep Enough**: Quality sleep is critical for both emotional and physical resilience. Lack of sleep can exacerbate stress, impair decision-making, and decrease emotional control. Prioritize sleep by maintaining a healthy bedtime routine and

ensuring that you're getting enough rest each night.

4. **Take Breaks**: When you feel overwhelmed, taking a break—whether it's a short walk, a weekend getaway, or simply stepping away from the situation for a few moments—can help clear your mind and restore your energy. Giving yourself permission to step back and recharge is essential to avoiding burnout.

How Self-Care Contributes to a Stronger Family

When family members prioritize self-care, they are better able to provide the emotional and practical support that their loved one in recovery needs. Healthy, well-balanced individuals are more emotionally available, better at setting boundaries, and more capable of maintaining patience and compassion in the face of challenges.

How Self-Care Strengthens the Family Unit:

1. **Improved Communication**: When you are emotionally healthy, you are better able to communicate effectively and empathetically with your loved ones. Self-care helps you regulate your emotions, making it easier to navigate difficult conversations and reduce conflicts.

2. **Greater Compassion**: Taking care of your own needs allows you to better understand and empathize with the struggles your loved one is facing in recovery. When you are physically and emotionally well, you can offer more compassionate support without becoming overwhelmed or resentful.

3. **Stronger Support for Your Loved One**: By practicing self-care, you can be a more consistent and reliable source of support. Your emotional resilience and strength will create a

stable foundation for your loved one to lean on during their recovery process.

4. **Healthier Family Dynamics**: A healthy family is one where each member feels valued, supported, and heard. When family members invest in their own well-being, it helps create a positive, nurturing atmosphere where everyone can thrive, including the person in recovery.

CHAPTER 14

DEVELOPING HEALTHY COMMUNICATION HABITS

Communication is the foundation of all healthy relationships, and it is especially important when a loved one is in recovery. Addiction always disrupts communication, causing serious misunderstandings, emotional distance and defensiveness. Developing healthy communication habits is crucial for rebuilding trust, resolving conflicts, and fostering a supportive environment for everyone involved. By learning to communicate with clarity, compassion, and respect, families can improve their relationships and create a healthier, more effective recovery process.

Solving the Problem of Misunderstandings and Arguments

Misunderstandings and arguments can arise

frequently in families dealing with addiction and recovery. Emotions are often heightened, and there may be deep-seated resentments or pain that needs to be addressed. However, it's essential to approach these challenges with patience and open-mindedness.

Common Causes of Misunderstandings:

1. **Expectations vs. Reality**: Family members may have expectations that recovery will be quick or smooth, which can lead to disappointment when setbacks occur. These unmet expectations can fuel arguments and frustration.

2. **Miscommunication**: The way people express their emotions or concerns can often lead to misunderstandings. One person might express anger or frustration, but the other may interpret it as criticism or rejection.

3. **Emotional Triggers**: Family members may unknowingly trigger emotional responses related to past hurts or trauma. These triggers can lead to

reactions that escalate into arguments rather than constructive dialogue.

How to Address Misunderstandings

Use "I" Statement: Instead of saying, "You never listen," try, "I feel unheard when..." This approach shifts the focus from blame to expressing your feelings constructively less likely to provoke defensiveness.

1. **Clarify Intentions**: If something is said that feels hurtful, ask for clarification rather than assuming the worst. For example, instead of assuming that someone is angry or frustrated, ask, "Can you explain what you meant by that?" This keeps misunderstandings from growing into larger problems.

2. **Take Time to Cool Off**: If a conversation is getting heated, agree to take a break and return to the discussion once everyone has calmed

down. This pause gives people time to reflect on their feelings and approach the conversation with a clearer mindset.

Learning to Speak and Listen with Compassion

Effective communication is not only about speaking clearly but also about listening attentively.. Compassionate listening and speaking can help create a safe, supportive space where everyone feels heard and understood. By learning to speak with kindness and listen with empathy, families can resolve conflicts, rebuild trust, and nurture the recovery process.

CHAPTER 15

CULTIVATING LONG-TERM HEALING AND CONNECTION

Recovery from addiction is often seen as a daunting and overwhelming process, not just for the person directly affected but for the entire family. It's common to focus intensely on the immediate goal of sobriety, managing cravings, and avoiding relapse. However, the true essence of recovery—both for the individual and the family—extends beyond the initial stages. It's about building a life that is connected, healthy and full in all aspects of life. Cultivating long-term healing and connection requires intention, patience, and a commitment to growth. For families, this means embracing life beyond the crisis of addiction, fostering unity and shared values, and celebrating every victory—no matter how small—along the way.

The process of recovery does not stop once sobriety is achieved; in fact, it is only the beginning of a new chapter. Long-term healing is about making sustainable changes that foster healthier relationships, emotional well-being, and shared goals. This chapter focuses on practical ways to cultivate healing and connection, drawing on compassion, mutual respect, and the continuous effort to strengthen bonds that have been tested over time.

How to Embrace Life beyond Recovery

For many families, addiction has been a pervasive, all-consuming experience. It shapes daily routines, impacts relationships, and often dictates the emotional tone of family life. Once recovery begins to take hold, there can be an unsettling feeling of what now? Both the individual in recovery and their family may feel uncertain and overwhelmed as they navigate their new reality. The challenge lies in embracing a life that is not centered around addiction or recovery struggles, but instead focuses on creating new routines, new values, and new goals.

The question is: how do you move forward, beyond the constant shadow of addiction, and build a life that feels normal, healthy, and fulfilling?

1. Redefine Your Family Identity

For years, addiction may have defined your family dynamic. It might have shaped how you interacted with each other, what roles everyone played, and what conversations were had—or avoided. Once recovery is underway, this old family identity will need to shift. You'll need to recognize and embrace new, healthier patterns of behavior and communication.

- **Step 1: Acknowledge the Past, but Focus on the Present**: Recognize that addiction may have impacted your family deeply, but don't let it become the lens through which you see your entire story. The past holds valuable lessons, but the present is where you have control and influence. Take stock of how far you've come and actively seek ways to create new memories that do not center around addiction.

- **Step 2: Open New Conversations**: Recovery is about opening up new lines of communication. This means letting go of old patterns where silence or tension might have prevailed. Start new conversations—whether they are about your hopes, dreams, or simply how your day went. Make room for lightness, laughter, and connection, even as you continue to heal.

- **Step 3: Create New Traditions**: Replacing old habits and routines is one way to feel that you're truly moving forward. Whether it's family dinners, game nights, weekend outings, or small rituals like a shared walk every evening, these traditions can become powerful symbols of growth and healing. They help reinforce the idea that your family is evolving in a positive direction.

2. Focus on Emotional Healing

Addiction leaves scars—not just on the person struggling with it, but on the whole family. The emotional wounds that result from betrayal, hurtful behavior, and damaged trust require time, patience, and active effort to heal. Embracing life beyond recovery means embracing the emotional work that is necessary for long-term wellness.

- **Step 1: Give Yourself Permission to Heal**: It's crucial for every family member to take the time to heal emotionally. This means allowing yourself to feel the pain of the past but also being kind enough to seek healing in the present. Therapy—both individual and family-based—can be a powerful tool in this emotional healing process. Therapy provides a safe, structured environment to work through past hurts and build new, healthier ways of interacting.

- **Step 2: Practice Self-Compassion**: Family members, just like the individual in recovery, need to be gentle with themselves. Healing from the trauma of addiction involves recognizing your own humanity and imperfections. Family members often carry guilt or shame for not being able to "fix" the situation sooner. However, healing happens when you stop blaming yourself and instead focus on supporting each other with empathy and understanding.

- **Step 3: Foster Forgiveness**: Forgiveness is a crucial element of long-term healing. While it doesn't mean excusing hurtful behavior, it's about releasing the emotional burden of holding on to anger and resentment. Family members who can forgive—not just the person who struggled with addiction, but also themselves—free themselves from the weight of the past and allow themselves to fully embrace the new chapter in their lives.

Fostering Unity and Positive Family Values

Addiction often divides families. It can pit members against each other, create misunderstandings, and cultivate feelings of betrayal or distrust. When recovery takes hold, one of the most powerful actions a family can take is to rebuild its foundation on unity and shared values. This is how families move from surviving addiction to thriving in a post-addiction reality.

1. Establish New Family Values

Values guide behavior and decisions, and they form the bedrock of healthy, connected families. Families who recover from addiction often find that they need to reestablish and re-align their values—what they believe in, how they interact with each other, and what their priorities are moving forward.

Step 1: Communicate Openly about Values: Have an open conversation with your family about what values are important moving forward. Is trust and honesty your highest priority? What about compassion, kindness, and forgiveness? As a family, make time to discuss what these values mean and how they can be reflected in your daily lives.

Step 2: Demonstrate healthy values: Let your actions reflect your principles. As a family, make it a point to consistently model the behaviors you want to see in each other. If honesty is one of your core values, be transparent with each other about your feelings and experiences. If respect is a cornerstone of your family, treat each other with dignity in every interaction.

Step 3: Reinforce Values in Daily Life: Values need to be lived, not just talked about. Whether it's offering emotional support during tough times, working together to meet shared goals, or simply showing appreciation for each other's efforts, practice these values every day. When family members see these values in action, they feel more secure and connected to one another.

2. Foster a culture grounded in accountability and responsibility.

Recovery and long-term healing require family members to take responsibility for their actions. This can be particularly important for those who have been hurt by addiction but must now rebuild trust. Accountability is essential for creating lasting change and unity within the family.

Step 1: Set Clear Expectations: As a family, agree on what's expected of each member in terms of behavior, communication, and support. Establish clear boundaries and ensure mutual understanding among everyone involved. For example, if one family member is in recovery, it's crucial to establish and respect boundaries related to their sobriety, as well as mutual respect in communication.

Step 2: Encourage Open Accountability: Accountability isn't about blaming or criticizing; it's about honest conversations regarding behavior and its impact. Hold each other accountable, but do so with care and respect. For example, if a family member makes a mistake or relapses, approach the conversation with empathy rather than judgment, emphasizing that recovery is an ongoing process.

Step 3: Celebrate Personal Growth: Accountability should be balanced with recognition of personal growth. Acknowledge and celebrate the positive steps that family members are taking, whether it's the individual in recovery attending therapy, a family member setting boundaries, or simply having a difficult but honest conversation. Encouragement promotes growth and reinforces unity.

CHAPTER 16

CELEBRATING SMALL VICTORIES AS A FAMILY

Healing and recovery aren't about dramatic, overnight changes. It's the small, consistent victories that matter most in the long term. The truth is, recovery is a process, not a destination. Celebrating these victories—however small—helps reinforce the progress being made and deepens family bonds.

1. Recognize Everyday Triumphs

Addiction recovery is a marathon, not a sprint, and sometimes the victories may seem small or insignificant. However, every step forward is a step toward recovery and connection. Whether it's a day without relapse, a difficult conversation being had with respect, or a family gathering free of tension, these moments are significant.

Step 1: Create a "Victory Wall" or Journal: One way to celebrate these small wins is by creating a tangible reminder of progress. You can start a victory wall or journal, where you write down and celebrate every accomplishment, no matter how minor it may seem. Seeing these victories in writing can be an incredibly affirming reminder of how far you've come.

Step 2: Celebrate Milestones Together: Celebrate important milestones in the recovery process—such as a certain number of sober days, a successful family therapy session, or the completion of a personal goal. These celebrations don't have to be grand; simple, meaningful gestures like a special dinner or a shared activity can go a long way in reinforcing the family's growth and unity.

2. Acknowledge Effort, Not Just Results

Sometimes, the energy is just as important as the results. While it's easy to focus only on the end goal (sobriety, emotional healing, etc.), the day-to-day commitment to growth deserves recognition. Even when the results aren't immediately visible, acknowledging effort fosters a sense of pride and accomplishment. It reinforces the idea that the process itself is valuable, not just the final result.

Step 1: Acknowledge Consistency: Sometimes, the most important victories come from consistent effort. This could mean showing up every day, sticking to a new routine, or confronting difficult emotions instead of avoiding them. These actions require courage and commitment, even if they don't produce instant results. By celebrating this consistency, you highlight the ongoing dedication to healing, regardless of how long it takes to see the effects.

Step 2: Celebrate Togetherness: Family unity is a victory in itself. Rebuilding trust, sharing meals without tension, or having a day where everyone gets along and feels heard—these are all signs of progress. They may not seem as monumental as overcoming addiction itself, but they are the foundation of long-term recovery and connection. By celebrating these moments, you reinforce the importance of family togetherness in the healing process.

3. **Create Rituals for Celebrating Milestones**: Establishing regular rituals for celebrating progress—whether it's a weekly reflection on successes or an annual family outing to mark milestones—helps solidify the habit of recognizing growth. These rituals can evolve over time, but they serve as a constant reminder that healing is a shared process, and every small step forward deserves recognition.

CONCLUSION

The effects of substance abuse stretch far beyond the individual; they ripple through families, communities, and loved ones. In **Substance Abuse Recovery Activities for Families,** we have seen how addiction doesn't just affect the person struggling with substance use—it affects every relationship and every individual within the family unit. But there is hope. Healing is possible, not only for the person directly impacted by addiction, but also for the family as a whole. It requires understanding, support, and above all, commitment to change.

Families are the cornerstone of recovery, and when they unite with a shared sense of purpose, they become an unbreakable force for positive change. This book emphasizes the importance of clear communication, healthy boundaries, and mutual respect in the healing process. It underscores the need for education, therapy, and counseling to address the emotional toll that addiction takes on everyone involved.

The road to recovery can be difficult, but through compassion and resilience, families can rebuild their connections, regain trust, and foster an environment of growth. By providing resources, strategies, and actionable steps, **Substance Abuse Recovery Activities for Families** offers a path forward—one where families are empowered to heal, reclaim their lives, and create lasting change. With patience, determination, and unwavering support for one another, recovery is not just a possibility, it's a promise.

www.ingramcontent.com/pod-product-compliance
Lightning Source LLC
Chambersburg PA
CBHW051612250726
48653CB00004BA/1479